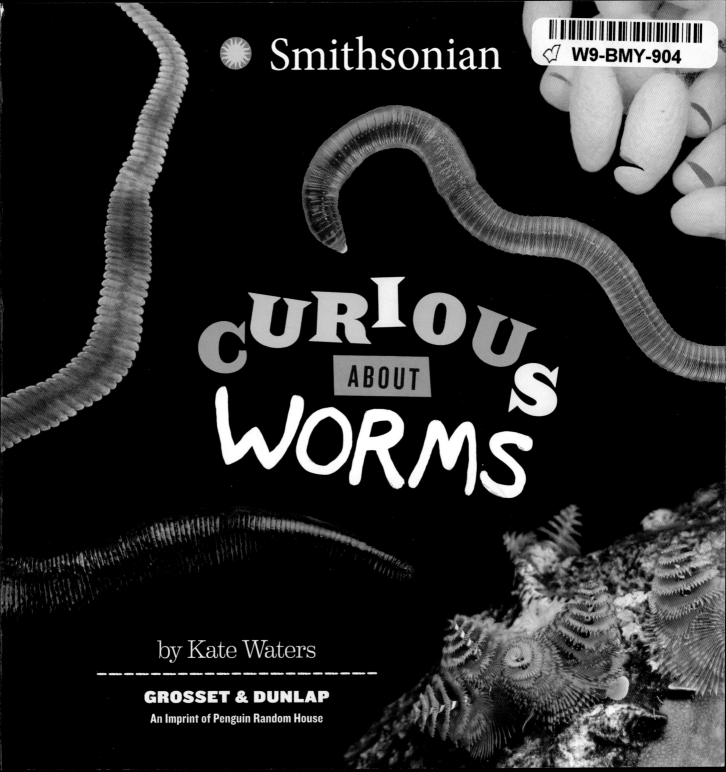

Smithsonian

CURIOUS
ABOUT
WORMS

by Kate Waters

GROSSET & DUNLAP

An Imprint of Penguin Random House

GROSSET & DUNLAP

Penguin Young Readers Group
An Imprint of Penguin Random House LLC

● Smithsonian

This trademark is owned by the Smithsonian Institution and
is registered in the U.S. Patent and Trademark Office.

Smithsonian Enterprises:
Christopher Liedel, President
Carol LeBlanc, Senior Vice President, Education and Consumer Products
Brigid Ferraro, Vice President, Education and Consumer Products
Ellen Nanney, Licensing Manager
Kealy Gordon, Product Development Manager

Smithsonian's National Museum of Natural History, Department of Invertebrate Zoology:
Dr. Jon L. Norenburg, Chairman, Research Zoologist
Dr. Karen Osborn, Research Zoologist, Curator of Peracarida and Polychaeta
Dr. Anna J. Phillips, Research Zoologist

PHOTO CREDITS: front cover (top right): Boonchuay_Promjiam/iStock/Thinkstock; front cover (top left), page 10:
K-Kucharska D-Kucharski/iStock/Thinkstock; front cover (middle right): pandemin/iStock/Thinkstock; front cover (bottom
right): hansgertbroeder/iStock/Thinkstock; front cover (bottom left), back cover (top): HeitiPaves/iStock/Thinkstock; back cover
(bottom right), page 1 (top center), pages 30–31 (center): bazilfoto/iStock/Thinkstock; back cover (bottom left), page 31 (bottom):
johnandersonphoto/iStock/Thinkstock; page 1 (top left), page 4 (top), page 30 (top left): Dr. Anna Phillips, Smithsonian National
Museum of Natural History; page 1 (bottom left), pages 6–7 (bottom), pages 30–31 (bottom): Vitalii Hulai/iStock/Thinkstock;
page 1 (top right), page 27 (top): piyagoon/iStock/Thinkstock; page 1 (bottom right), page 20: G. P. Schmahl, NOAA FGBNMS
Manager; page 3: Henry Kaiser/National Science Foundation; page 4 (bottom): NOAA Okeanos Explorer Program, Gulf of Mexico 2012
Expedition; page 5 (top): Smithsonian Environmental Research Institute; page 5 (bottom): NOAA; page 6 (left), page 11 (bottom):
ConstantinCornel/iStock/Thinkstock; page 7 (top), page 31 (top): toeytoey2530/iStock/Thinkstock; pages 8–9: Bruno C. Vellutini/
Wikimedia Commons (CC BY-SA 3.0); page 11 (top): MyImages_Micha/iStock/Thinkstock; page 12 (top): shauni/iStock/Thinkstock;
page 12 (bottom): Vitaliy Pakhnyushchyy/Hemera/Thinkstock; page 13: Bernhard Richter/iStock/Thinkstock; page 14: Pieria/
Wikimedia Commons; page 15: Bernard DUPONT/Wikimedia Commons (CC BY-SA 2.0); page 16: NOAA Okeanos Explorer Program,
Mid-Cayman Rise Expedition 2011; page 17 (top): NOAA Okeanos Explorer Program; page 17 (bottom): University of Washington,
NOAA/OAR/OER; page 18: Pierre Gros/Wikimedia Commons (CC BY 4.0) (background removed); page 19: Guido Bohne/Wikimedia
Commons (CC BY-SA 2.0); page 21: vilainecrevette/iStock/Thinkstock; page 22, page 23 (left): selvanegra/iStock/Thinkstock;
page 23 (right): Smithsonian National Museum of Natural History; page 24: Ablestock.com/Thinkstock; page 25: PhillDanze/iStock/
Thinkstock; page 26: Henrik_L/iStock/Thinkstock; page 27 (bottom): Laures/iStock/Thinkstock; page 28 (top): ironman 100/iStock/
Thinkstock; page 28 (bottom): Ian_Redding/iStock/Thinkstock; page 29: mpalmer/iStock/Thinkstock; page 32: NOAA.

ISBN 9780451533692   10 9 8 7 6 5 4 3

What can wriggle underground, sway in the ocean, or even live at the South Pole?

WORMS!

Worms live in every environment on earth. You'll find them in deserts, forests, grasslands, tundra, and both freshwater and saltwater. Some worms even live on or inside animals.

Worm from inside a bird

Worms in ice

Worms in dirt

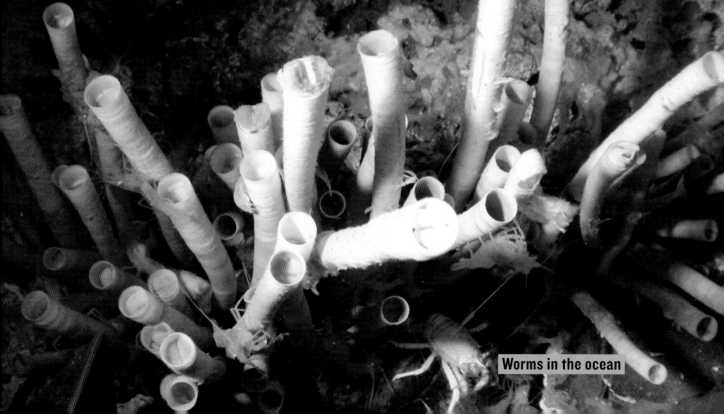
Worms in the ocean

There are millions of
species of worms.
Segmented worms have
body parts that repeat
in a pattern you can see.
Earthworms and leeches
are segmented worms.
A flatworm gets its name
from its shape. Tapeworms
are flatworms.

Close-up of segments

Leech

Roundworms have round, smooth bodies with no segments. Many of these worms are tiny and hard to see. Most of them are transparent. Some roundworms are parasites. They live inside other animals and can grow quite large.

Worms can range in size from very small to very long. The smallest is 1/64 of an inch. Your ruler doesn't even have a line for things that small! Scientists look at those worms with microscopes.

The longest worms can reach 165 feet. That is as long as three and a half school buses in a line. The longest worms may also be the oldest. Some can be more than 100 years old.

This worm is about six feet long.
It can stretch to more than sixty feet!

If you say "worm," most people think of earthworms. These segmented worms live wherever there is soil.

An earthworm has muscles along its entire body. These muscles and tiny **bristles** help it move.

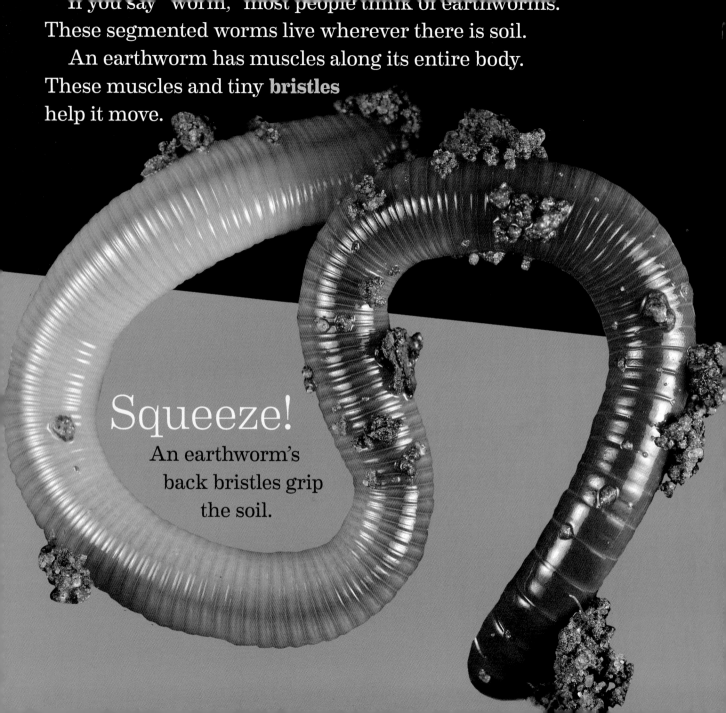

Squeeze!
An earthworm's back bristles grip the soil.

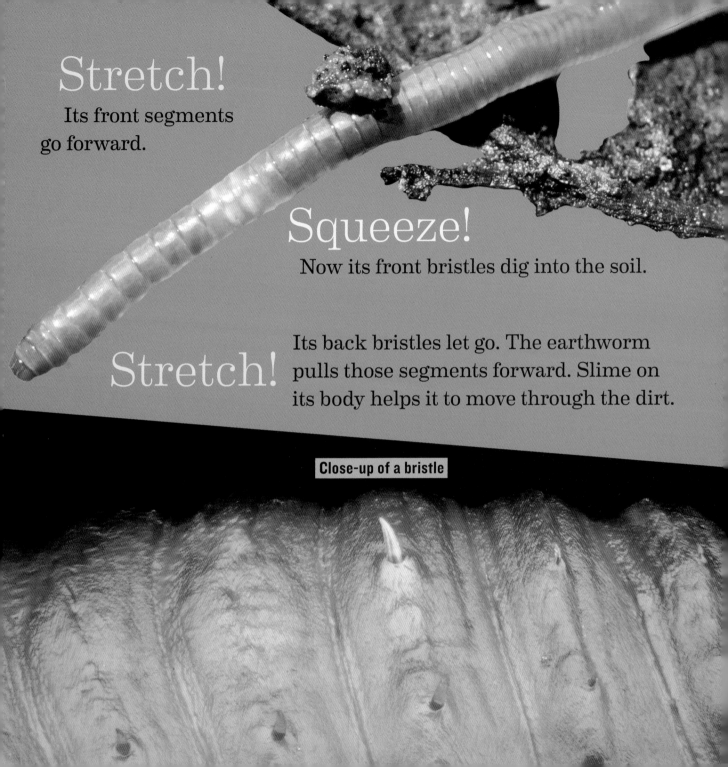

Stretch!

Its front segments go forward.

Squeeze!

Now its front bristles dig into the soil.

Stretch!

Its back bristles let go. The earthworm pulls those segments forward. Slime on its body helps it to move through the dirt.

Close-up of a bristle

Earthworms can dig down as far as six feet. As they burrow in the soil, they eat the dirt, dead plants, and leaves. They leave behind waste material after they digest their food. This digging and worm waste is good for the soil.

Earthworms like dark, moist environments. They breathe through their skin which has to stay moist. You will not see live earthworms in the sunlight unless you lift up a rock or dig into the soil. They do not live in the dry, hot desert or in places where the ground is always frozen.

Earthworms and their waste, which is called castings.

A land leech is another kind of segmented worm.
It lives in areas of the world that are warm and moist.
A land leech only eats one thing: blood.
It hides in leaves or on the forest floor and
waits for a **mammal** to pass under it or
brush against it.
Then it makes its move!

The leech's strong suckers attach
it to its mammal **host**. Two or three
jaws at its front end cut into the
animal. The host doesn't
even feel the worm that
is drinking its blood!

Land leech

Land leech after eating

A land leech feeds for about ten to thirty minutes. It **swells** until it's ten times bigger and drops off the animal. It doesn't need to eat again for several weeks.

Deep down on the ocean floor, there are openings where hot water shoots out. The water has been heated deep inside the earth. Giant tube worms live around these **vents** or openings. The hose-shaped worms attach one end of their tubes to the ocean floor.

Tube worm near a vent

The rest of their tube bodies, which can be ten feet long, sway in the water. Tube worms have **bacteria** living inside them. These bacteria change liquids coming out of the vents into food for the worms.

Giant red tube worms on a vent

Flatworms can also live in the ocean. They look like wavy leaves floating along the ocean floor. When this worm finds a snail, it curls around it. The flatworm shoots liquid into the snail to break it down into food.

Flatworm eating a snail

Ribbon worm

Ribbon worms are long and thin. They have a body part that shoots out and wraps around anything they want to eat.

There are thousands of kinds of bristle worms in the ocean. They live in the top, middle, and bottom layers of the water. Bristle worms have sharp stiff hairs that stick out from their body segments. These bristles help the worm swim, crawl, and dig to hide in the sand. They also provide protection from other animals. Bristle worms are hard to swallow!

Feather duster worms are a kind of bristle worm. They build tubes and then live inside. The tubes are attached to things on the ocean floor, like corals. The worms' feathery **tentacles** catch small creatures and other food swimming by.

Christmas tree bristle worms

Feather duster worm

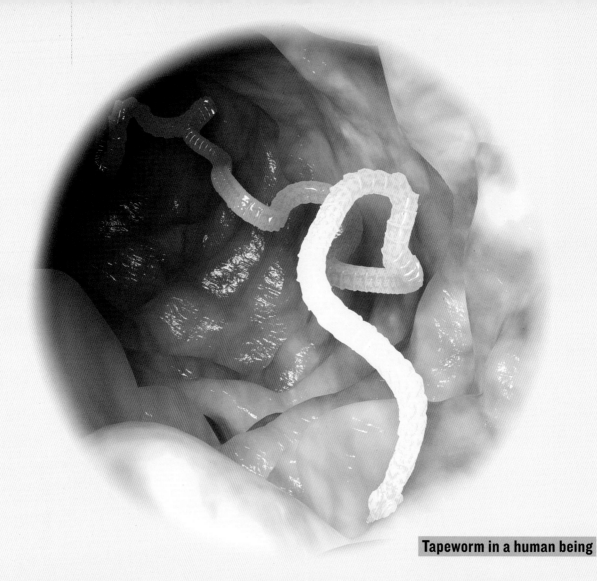

Tapeworm in a human being

A tapeworm is a parasite. This flatworm lives inside other animal hosts. Its body has two parts. One part has suckers or hooks or both! They grab onto the insides of the host. The long, main part takes in food from the host. Tapeworms live in many kinds of land animals— even people!

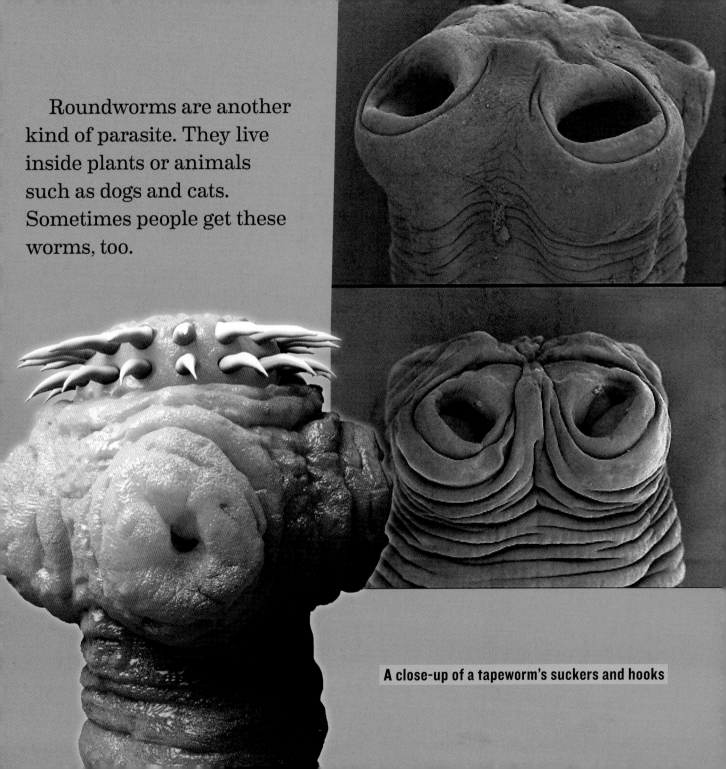

Roundworms are another kind of parasite. They live inside plants or animals such as dogs and cats. Sometimes people get these worms, too.

A close-up of a tapeworm's suckers and hooks

Worms are food for other animals such as birds, fish, toads, mice, and raccoons. Worms have to be quick to escape being eaten. Earthworms use their strong muscles to dig into the ground with amazing speed. Many ocean worms make themselves taste bad so they won't get eaten.

Worms in a compost bin

People use worms, too. Earthworms are good bait for fishing. Worms help turn leftover food into rich **compost** to put in a garden. In some countries people cook and eat worms.

Glow worms,
silkworms, and
inchworms all sound
like kinds of worms.
But they're not!

A glow worm is an
insect that glows at
its rear end.

A silkworm is an early stage of a moth. It spins a **cocoon**. That material is used to make silk thread.

An inchworm is also the young form of a moth. It will prepare a cocoon and turn into a moth.

Some wiggly questions about worms:

If you cut an earthworm in half, will both parts grow back?

No. It may regrow a small tail end, depending on where it was cut. Or it will just die.

Why do earthworms come out of the ground when it rains?

Don't worry! They won't drown in the ground when it rains. Earthworms come out then because the surface of the earth is wet. They can travel above ground. On sunny days, their skin would dry out. The worms then wouldn't be able to breathe.

How can an earthworm tell if it's going up or down in the soil?
One end of an earthworm's body is sensitive to light. It knows
when it is getting close to the surface of the ground.

People often call living things by different names. But scientists use one naming system to keep track of information. Living things that are related to one another and have similar features are grouped together. Every living thing is given a scientific name in the Latin language. This way scientists all over the world know which animal or plant other scientists are talking about!

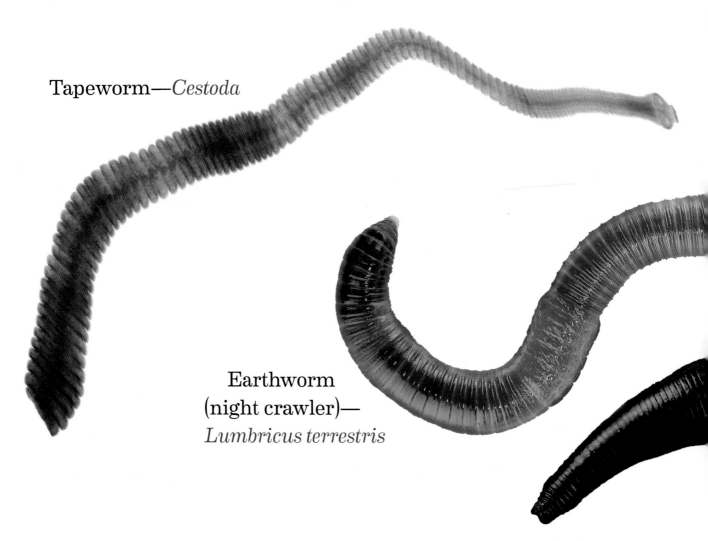

Tapeworm—*Cestoda*

Earthworm (night crawler)— *Lumbricus terrestris*

Here are some of the many types of worms. Their scientific names are in red.

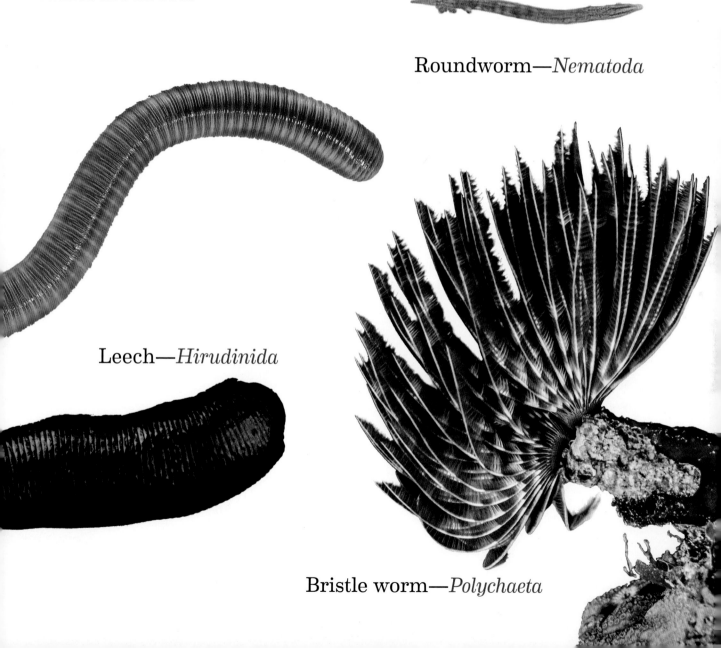

Roundworm—*Nematoda*

Leech—*Hirudinida*

Bristle worm—*Polychaeta*

bacteria: microscopic living things that exist all around and inside you

bristles: stiff body hairs

burrow: to dig (verb); a hole in the ground where an animal lives (noun)

castings: worms' waste material

cocoon: a covering some animals make for protection

compost: a mixture of leftover food, leaves, and waste material that breaks down and then can be added to soil to make it rich

digest: to break down food so it can be used by the body

host: an animal or plant that is home or food for a parasite

mammal: a warm-blooded animal

parasite: a living thing that lives on or in another animal or plant

segmented: divided into repeated parts

species: a group of animals or plants that are similar and can produce young animals or plants

swells: becomes bigger for a time

tentacles: an animal's long arms

transparent: clear or see-through

tundra: a flat area where the land is always frozen

vents: openings on the ocean floor